THE
BATTLE
of
GETTYSBURG

A HISTORY PERSPECTIVES BOOK

Roberta Baxter

Published in the United States of America by Cherry Lake Publishing
Ann Arbor, Michigan
www.cherrylakepublishing.com

Consultants: Peter C. Vermilyea, Lecturer, History Department, Western
Connecticut State University; Marla Conn, ReadAbility, Inc.
Editorial direction: Red Line Editorial
Book design and illustration: Sleeping Bear Press

Photo Credits: David C. Bettison/Library of Congress, cover (left), 1 (left);
Library of Congress, cover (middle), 1 (middle), 4, 11, 14, 17, 25, 28, 30;
Anthony Berger/Library of Congress, cover (right), 1 (right), 6; North
Wind/North Wind Picture Archives, 8, 19, 21, 23; Townsend & Broas/
Library of Congress, 22

Library of Congress Cataloging-in-Publication Data
Baxter, Roberta, 1952-
  The Battle of Gettysburg / Roberta Baxter.
    pages cm. – (Perspectives library)
  ISBN 978-1-62431-415-5 (hardcover) – ISBN 978-1-62431-491-9 (pbk.)
– ISBN 978-1-62431-453-7 (pdf) – ISBN 978-1-62431-529-9 (ebook)
1. Gettysburg, Battle of, Gettysburg, Pa., 1863–Juvenile literature. I. Title.
E475.53.B35 2013
973.7'349–dc23
                        2013006434

Cherry Lake Publishing would like to acknowledge the work of
The Partnership for 21st Century Skills. Please visit www.p21.org
for more information.

Printed in the United States of America
Corporate Graphics Inc.
July 2013
CLFA11

TABLE OF CONTENTS

In this book, you will read about the Battle of Gettysburg, which took place during the American Civil War. Each perspective is based on real things that happened to real people who experienced the battle. As you'll see, the same event can look different depending on one's point of view.

Albert Schmidt

Union Soldier

My fellow soldiers and I have been fighting this civil war since it began two years ago in 1861. The South wanted us to accept their rights to own slaves, but many in the North believe no man should own another. In 1861, several Southern states **seceded** from the United States to form their own country, the Confederate States of America, or the **Confederacy** for short.

Our founders fought and died to form this country in the 1770s. Now the Southerners want to break it up.

President Abraham Lincoln believes the **Union** should stay joined. He said if the country were divided, it would fall. He wants all the states to remain part of the United States. So when he called for soldiers, many of us came from Milwaukee, Wisconsin, to fight to preserve the Union. Other boys from Michigan and Indiana **enlisted** too. We are a unit called the Iron Brigade because we are some of the strongest fighters in this army.

We've fought the **rebels** several times, and many of those battles we lost. They are fierce fighters. We've marched over this country in sun and rain to fight for our Union. Last year, 1862, General Robert E. Lee led the Confederates in an invasion of the North. We beat them at a battle in Maryland near Antietam Creek on September 17. But we lost a couple battles after that.

*◀ President Abraham Lincoln wanted
the Union to stay together.*

Our spirits were low, and we
weren't sure how this war
would turn out.

The rebels invaded us again
on June 15, 1863. They marched
north into Pennsylvania. We
learned President Lincoln thought
they might attack Washington, so we marched toward
the city. No one knew exactly where the rebels were,
but we hoped to find them and push them out of
our land. We had a new commander, General George
Meade. He was said to be a tough fighter, so we were
ready to fight if it came to that.

We later learned both armies had been marching
north on either side of the same mountains. On July 1,
our **cavalry** saw the rebels. We were near a small,

pretty town in Pennsylvania called Gettysburg. The rebels attacked with their **artillery** and our boys were pinned down. Our commander ordered some of our boys of the Iron Brigade to attack the rebels through a patch of woods outside of the town. The rebels didn't know they were up against the best **infantry** in the whole Union army. Slowly our men pushed forward, forcing the rebels right out of those woods. Some of them surrendered. One of our boys even captured a Confederate general.

The rest of the Iron Brigade, including myself, was sent to join a group of Union soldiers who were fighting on the side of a road about half a mile out of Gettysburg. We marched forward into a withering fire of bullets. Men all around me were going down, but I had no time to see who. We were firing at an enemy we could barely see through the gun smoke. The noise from the cannon and rifle fire was so loud I could barely hear a man next to me, even if he yelled.

The smoke was so thick that I could barely find a target for my next shot. My throat was burning from the smoke, but I had no time for a swig of water. As I climbed over a fence, I felt a tug at my coat and I lost my hat. I grabbed my hat and moved forward. Later, I found bullet holes in both my coat and hat.

▲ *The battlefields at Gettysburg were very loud.*

I heard our Lieutenant Colonel Rufus Dawes yelling, "Forward! Forward!" Even through the noise of the battle, I could hear him yelling. Others started hollering, and I was hollering too. We pushed ahead through the smoke and bullets and surrounded the rebels. Lieutenant Colonel Dawes yelled for the group to surrender, and they did. But that was only around 230 of the thousands of rebels fighting.

SECOND SOURCE

▶ Find another source on this battle from a Union soldier's point of view and compare the information there to the information in this source. How are they different? How are they similar?

After that fight, we were ordered to guard an artillery unit. We could see the fight was going on all around Gettysburg. The town has about 2,400 residents, but thankfully most were hiding during the battle. With all the smoke, it was hard to see who was winning. Our unit had a lot of men killed or wounded on that first day. It was a huge blow to our forces. We knew the battle would continue the next day, and we had to do better if we were going to win.

On the next day, July 2, there were fights all over the farmland around Gettysburg. It really took hold of us that we were fighting on our soil. Even though we won the Battle of Antietam in Maryland last September, fighting there was not the same as fighting here. Maryland is still a slave state. Pennsylvania is a free Northern state, and we needed to defend it with all our might.

Many brave Union boys lost their lives in a pile of huge rocks called Devil's Den. Later, I heard about some courageous Maine soldiers who fought on a hill called Little Round Top. It's about two miles south of the town of Gettysburg. The Maine boys were running out of bullets, and they were getting desperate. They charged the rebels with their bayonets. It was an incredibly risky move, but they held their position on the hill. Other boys fought the rebels in a wheat field. The wheat was trampled into the dirt. One man I met said there were so many bodies you could barely see the ground. By the end of the day, we had fought off the Confederates but had lost hundreds of men. I was sure they would attack again the next day.

On July 3, we were exhausted from the fighting. The morning was fairly quiet. Then just after midday,

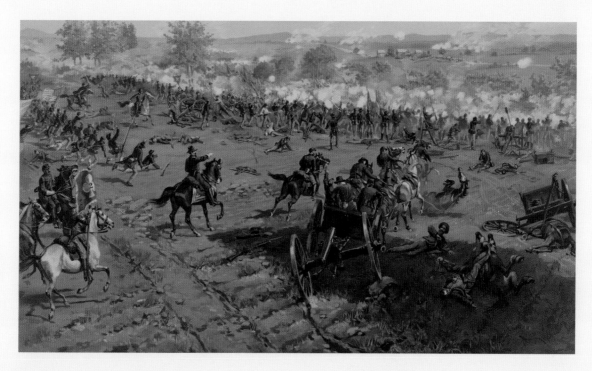

▲ *After a rough start, the Union army won the Battle of Gettysburg.*

the artillery of both sides started again. There were so many artillery shells in the air we could barely see anything. The earth shook, and no one could hear anything but the guns.

A large group of rebels charged against the center of one of our lines. The Union troops that witnessed the battle said it was a horrible sight to see. Our boys

TURNING POINT OF THE WAR

The Battle of Gettysburg was the turning point of the American Civil War. Before it, the Confederates were at an advantage, having won some key battles. But, about one-third of the Confederate soldiers who fought at Gettysburg died. After the battle, the Confederate army was weakened and no longer the threat it had once been.

beat the Confederates back across the battlefield. More than 4,000 rebels died, and we held our position. That attack took all the fight out of the rebels.

We Union men won this battle, but it was at an almost unbearable cost of men. Today, on July 4, the very birthday of our great country, the Confederate army **retreated** from Gettysburg. I wish they would stop fighting, give up their slaves, and be a part of our Union again. We could all celebrate our nation's Independence Day together instead of killing one another.

THINK ABOUT IT

▶ Determine the main point of this chapter. Pick out two pieces of evidence that support that point.

Samuel Thorpe

Confederate Soldier

In late June 1863, I was in Pennsylvania with General Robert E. Lee's Confederate army. The rumor was we were marching into the state to get supplies. This land had not yet faced war. The fields and orchards were full of wheat and apples. Chickens and pigs could be seen in the barnyards. This was very different from the battlegrounds we'd marched through in the South.

Some said General Lee was hoping to beat the **Yankees** in a big battle up here in their territory. Then they would settle for peace and leave us alone in our new country, the Confederate States of America. When we accomplish that, I can go home.

I've been fighting this war so we Southerners can keep our rights to own slaves. The Northerners don't want any part of slavery. But why does that mean they should take our rights away? Besides that, President Lincoln and the federal government cannot tell the states what to do. The job of the federal government is to defend the country and make treaties with other countries. It needs to leave the states alone. This is what I believe, and that is why I enlisted to defend my home and my state of North Carolina. But I didn't think we would be invading the

ANALYZE THIS

▶ Analyze the reasons behind the war in the first and second chapters. How are the perspectives different? How are they the same?

North. It's one thing to defend your land, but it's something else to attack another outright. I'm still not sure if it was the right thing to do.

We met the Yankee army on July 1, just as we came into a town called Gettysburg. Roads from all over Pennsylvania lead into the town, so it made sense that we met each other there. At the beginning of the battle, I heard fellow soldiers say that if our Confederacy could beat them here, President Lincoln would have no choice but to stop the war. But today is July 4, 1863, and the battle did not go as we hoped. We fought for three days against strong Yankee battle lines. Those were the longest and toughest three days of my life.

On July 1, the battle started outside of the town. Throughout the day, we pushed the Yankees back so that they ran right through the town and into the hilly farmland to the south. Once they got out of town, they dug trenches into the hills. We fired from behind trees and fences, trying to hit any target we could find until it was too dark to see anything. By the end of the day, we had done much damage to the Yankee army. We were certain a victory was within our grasp.

The next day, my unit was ordered to attack up a hill known as Cemetery Ridge. Yankee soldiers were at the top. The hill is aptly named, as we left

▲ *The Confederate army believed it was positioned to win the Battle of Gettysburg.*

many bodies on that ground. The noise from the muskets and cannon was unbelievable. The smoke was so thick I could scarcely breathe. At some point during the fighting, I was wounded in my left upper arm, and it became hard to raise my rifle. Once we were back at the camp for the night, I had it bandaged. I wanted to continue the fight, but the captain said I was to stay out of the way, as I wouldn't be much help.

On July 3, I sat under a tree near our field hospital and watched the battle at Cemetery Ridge. In the early afternoon, our artillery started firing and theirs fired back. The Yankees were massed on Cemetery Ridge and our boys were going to try to take it. Our infantry advanced. General George Pickett led the advance, and I hear they are now calling this Pickett's Charge.

SECOND SOURCE

▶ Find another source telling the story of Gettysburg from a Confederate soldier's point of view. Compare the information there to the information in this source.

It was the bloodiest, most foolish waste of good men I have ever seen. Our men marched shoulder to shoulder, with guns at the ready and flags flying high, through an open field toward Yankee lines. The Yankee artillery began shooting at them. I could see groups of our men fall while the others advanced around them to fill their spots. Then thousands of Yankees fired from behind the top of the ridge. Our boys in gray fell in fast numbers. I couldn't hear my voice, but I realized I was yelling. It pained me to see them go down. Next, our boys were in retreat. No one could stand against that awful wall of bullets. More than half of the men who charged died during that advance.

Pickett's Charge led to a huge loss of Confederate troops. ▶

As the exhausted men returned to camp, General Lee was there to meet them and take the blame himself. He had ordered the charge. He believed the center of the Union lines was weak. He thought the Union troops would retreat, leading to a Confederate victory. But he was terribly wrong and blamed himself for the slaughter.

Toward the end of July 3, many of our wounded were loaded onto wagons to be carried out of the

NUMBER OF CASUALTIES

Nearly 160,000 soldiers fought at the Battle of Gettysburg. About 51,000 men were killed or wounded in the battle. It was the bloodiest battle of the American Civil War. More than one-third of General Lee's troops that fought at Gettysburg were killed or wounded. The South was unable to recover from these heavy losses.

town. We had so many wounded that the wagon train stretched 17 miles long. The rain poured down in sheets. I thought of the fields that we had left stained with blood. Perhaps the rain would wash it away.

The rest of us are starting our march back to the South today, July 4. There may be more battles ahead, and I shall fight as I am able. I am anxious for the war to be over and for me to return home, whatever the outcome may be.

◀ *Thousands of wounded Confederate troops retreated from Gettysburg after the battle was over.*

Anna Parker

Owner of General Store in Gettysburg

In the summer of 1863, my husband, John, was in Mississippi with the Union army of General Ulysses S. Grant. John agrees with President Lincoln's belief that the Union needs to stay together. But now the war has come to us, and he is far away.

I have been trying to keep our store in our town of Gettysburg in business so he will have a business to come home to. Since the war began, I've been struggling with the increase in prices for goods. My customers can hardly pay these high prices. I can no longer buy and sell some items, such as cotton cloth, because it is so expensive.

Then on June 26, 1863, our son William called out that soldiers were coming down the street. I rushed out and saw a few Confederate soldiers. They were the sorriest group I have ever seen. Most wore only rags and no shoes. The soldiers I met were polite, but I heard their commander demanded that Gettysburg give the soldiers goods, such as shoes and food. How could our little town afford to do that? Some tried to buy goods from my store, but I told them I could not accept their Confederate paper money.

Some Confederate soldiers came into the town of Gettysburg before the battle began. ▶

They dared to secede from our Union and fight against their own brothers and friends. The soldiers left town, so I'm guessing they must have just been seeing what supplies we had.

On July 1, the soldiers were back. This time there were both Confederate and Union soldiers. They began fighting around our quiet town. When I heard the sound of gunfire early that morning, I gathered up the children and we fled to the cellar. The noise was fearsome. We waited in the darkness, hearing the booms and feeling the ground shake. I tried to be brave for the children, but I was scared. Would they be coming into town? What if our home was destroyed in the fighting?

The soldiers were fighting north of town, and I hoped they wouldn't come nearer to us.

ANALYZE THIS

▶ Compare Anna Parker's experience of the battle to one of the soldier's perspectives. How are the perspectives similar? How are they different?

Around noon that day, I crept up the cellar stairs to check on the store. The noise was so vicious I did not take the time to check our family area above the store. Later in the afternoon, a group of rebels chased some Union troops down our street. I had come up to check on the store again. I hid when I heard their rough voices, but they hurried past.

▲ *Gettysburg residents heard the noise from the battlefield.*

When night came, the battle stopped. The children and I came upstairs for a quick wash and I hastily gathered some food for dinner. Then I made them return to the cellar in case the fighting began again. I hid my husband's revolver in my sewing basket and kept it nearby. If anyone had come down the cellar stairs to threaten us, I would have shot them.

Most of July 2 passed quietly. A neighbor, Mr. Birch, came asking for supplies to care for wounded soldiers. I gave them to him without charge. He said they might need my help later, but for now, I should tend to my children.

In the afternoon, the shooting began again. Mostly it was south of the town. We wondered about our friends who live on farms in that area. I could hear gunfire into the night.

On July 3, the battle raged again to the south. Mr. Birch came asking for help with the wounded. He helped four Union soldiers into the store, and we stretched them out on the floor. I did what I could to comfort them, clean their wounds, and give them water and food. It was awful to see those brave men suffer. Why should they be shot because Southerners think it is their right to own slaves? Why couldn't the South rejoin the Union and end this war?

On July 4, there was no more fighting. The battle was over, and the soldiers of both sides left. Any soldiers who remain in Gettysburg are the dead who must be buried or the wounded who must be cared for. Some army doctors are still here, caring for the wounded. The Union army buried hundreds, both Union and Confederate troops, in long trenches. Later, men were paid to dig those bodies up, identify them as best they could, and bury them in a national cemetery.

THINK ABOUT IT

▶ Determine the main point of this chapter and pick out two pieces of evidence that support it.

▲ *President Lincoln's Gettysburg Address has become one of the most famous speeches in U.S. history.*

It has been several months since the battle near our town. Today, on November 19, 1863, President Abraham Lincoln spoke in Gettysburg to dedicate the new cemetery. He talked about the sacrifice of those who gave the last full measure of devotion. His speech was short, and I remember the ending words—that government of the people, by the people, and for the people shall not perish from the earth.

I pray that my John is home soon and no longer sacrificing for our Union.

THE GETTYSBURG ADDRESS

President Lincoln came to Gettysburg to dedicate a cemetery for soldiers from both sides. Edward Everett, a well-known speaker, talked for two hours, and then Lincoln spoke. He spoke for about two minutes and said 272 words. Yet, those words of the Gettysburg Address are some of the most famous in U.S. history.

LOOK, LOOK AGAIN

This illustration shows the fighting at the Battle of Gettysburg. Use this image to answer the following questions:

1. What would a Union soldier say is happening in this scene?

2. How would a Confederate soldier describe this scene in a letter to his family?

3. If a civilian resident of Gettysburg were to see this scene, what would he or she notice?

GLOSSARY

artillery (ahr-TIL-ur-ee) large guns mounted on carts

cavalry (KAV-uhl-ree) the part of an army that fought while on horses

Confederacy (kuhn-FED-ur-uh-see) the 11 Southern states that declared independence from the United States before the American Civil War

enlist (en-LIST) to join a military group

infantry (IN-fuhn-tree) soldiers who march and fight on foot

rebel (REB-uhl) a name used by Union soldiers for those in the Confederacy

retreat (ri-TREET) to pull back or withdraw from a battlefield

secede (si-SEED) to formally leave a group, such as the Union

Union (YOON-yuhn) the Northern states that stayed loyal to the United States during the American Civil War

Yankee (YANG-kee) a name used by Confederate soldiers for those in the Union

LEARN MORE

Further Reading

Fradin, Dennis Brindell. *The Battle of Gettysburg.* New York: Marshall Cavendish Benchmark, 2008.

Putnam, Jeff. *A Nation Divided: Causes of the Civil War.* New York: Crabtree, 2011.

Weber, Jennifer L. *Summer's Bloodiest Days: The Battle of Gettysburg as Told from All Sides.* Washington, DC: National Geographic, 2010.

Web Sites

Civil War
http://www.brainpop.com/socialstudies/freemovies/civilwar/
Here readers can read information and watch videos about topics such as the causes of the American Civil War, slavery, and more.

Gettysburg National Military Park
http://www.nps.gov/gett/forkids/index.htm
This Web site includes information and photos of the Gettysburg National Military Park.

INDEX

ABOUT THE AUTHOR

Roberta Baxter has written about history and science for students of all ages. She has written about the American Civil War in *The Northern Home Front of the Civil War*, *The Southern Home Front of the Civil War*, and *Battles for Gold and Glory: Civil War Skirmishes in New Mexico Territory*.